PEACE
PRAYERS
FROM THE WORLD'S FAITHS

ROGER GRAINGER

First published by O Books, 2006
O Books is an imprint of John Hunt Publishing Ltd.,
The Bothy, Deershot Lodge, Park Lane,
Ropley, Hants, SO24 0BE, UK
office1@o-books.net
www.o-books.net

Distribution in:
UK and Europe
Orca Book Services
orders@orcabookservices.co.uk
Tel: 01202 665432 Fax: 01202 666219 Int. code (44)

USA and Canada
NBN
custserv@nbnbooks.com
Tel: 1 800 462 6420 Fax: 1 800 338 4550

Australia
Brumby Books
sales@brumbybooks.com
Tel: 61 3 9761 5535 Fax: 61 3 9761 7095

Singapore
STP
davidbuckland@tlp.com.sg
Tel: 65 6276 Fax: 65 6276 7119

South Africa
Alternative Books
altbook@peterhyde.co.za
Tel: 27 011 792 7730 Fax: 27 011 792 7787

Text copyright Roger Grainger 2006

Design and cover photograph: Stuart Davies

ISBN-13: 978 1 905047 66 6
ISBN-10: 1 905047 66 5

A CIP catalogue record for this book is available from the British Library.

Printed in the US by Maple Vail

PEACE
PRAYERS

FROM THE WORLD'S FAITHS

ROGER GRAINGER

Edited by the WPWP Committee

BOOKS

Winchester, UK
Washington, USA

CONTENTS

**In loving memory of
Sidney Hinkes**

Introduction

Although it was a Christian Initiative that led to the founding of the Week of Prayer for World Peace in 1974, it soon became an interfaith activity. Our first Chairman, the late Dr Edward Carpenter, Former Dean of Westminster, established the guiding principle of the Week in the words "The Peace of the world must be prayed for by the faiths of the world", and this is still the basis of our work today.

For those who want to persevere with the idea of praying with people of other faiths, three thoughts may be helpful. First, the different prayers that we say are said by neighbours in the same town and the same street every week. In worshipping together we simply bring under one roof what happens anyway under the same sky. Secondly, we are convinced that there is only one humanity that prays, and only one Divinity that we pray to, whatever different opinions we may have about that one Divinity. Thirdly, we recognise that inter-faith partnership does not itself imply agreement. The things we agree on are many, and precious. The things we disagree on are precious too. When we stand with a follower of another faith who is praying, whenever we can agree with the prayer, we give it our interior assent. Where we cannot agree, we withhold our interior assent. It is still good to stand with that person as a friend and as a partner for peace.

Sidney Hinkes

Preface

People sometimes say that religion causes wars, and that without it we would all of us live together in peace. The Week of Prayer for World Peace, organised by eight world religions to pray for peace and reconciliation in a world torn apart by war, proves the cliché false. Here, different religions join together IN peace FOR peace. The aim of the group is to bring home as powerfully and vividly as possible the love that is God and the horror that is war. Thus it is not only inner peace – tranquillity of mind and soul – which is being sought here, but an end to agony and bloodshed, physical and psychological torture, abuse of every kind, taking place in the world of men, women, children and animals. This is an intensely practical prayer book, one that is earthed in the pain of being human.

The prayers come from (at least) nine traditions, yet they all reveal the same loathing for war. It is this that brought the group together; this, and humanity's deep need to bring its sorrows to God. Peace itself comes in many different forms, and the book has been arranged to be as flexible and comprehensive as we could make it. It consists of eight 'weeks' of prayer, each of them containing eight 'days' of prayer and intercessions on themes concerning peace – the format of the yearly Week of Prayer for World Peace pamphlets, in fact.

The religions of the world pray separately for peace.

Sometimes, though, they manage to pray together.

This book contains some of the evidence.

Roger Grainger

Week One

Sharing
Caring
Acting Justly
Stewarding
Honouring
Working Against War
Easing Burdens
Nurturing

1. Sharing

The righteous give generously

(Psalm 37 v 21)

Inspire us, O Wise Lord, to live in mutual understanding and trust and peace. We are brothers and sisters, all belonging to one great human family and we are children of one Father - Thou, O Wise Lord teach us to live as comrades, all in willing fellowship and loving fraternity, in brotherly and sisterly helpfulness and co-operation.

(Zoroastrian)

We pray for:
- Greater understanding of human interdependence
- communities that are divided among themselves
- groups of people of different racial or religious back grounds living next to one another
- all who seek to heal ancient wounds
- those who still cling to old bitterness

May God betide all people. May the sovereign rule the earth, following the righteous paths. May all beings ever attain what is good. May the worlds be prosperous and happy.

(Hindu, Vedic Hymn)

Gladden our hearts through the fragrance of your love.
Brighten our eyes through the light of your guidance.
Delight our ears through the melody of your work and shelter us all in the stronghold of your providence, for you have created all humanity and have decreed that we shall all belong to the same household.

(Baha'i)

2. Caring

Your rod and your staff, they comfort me

(Psalm 23 v 4)

We remember the grace and blessings of Allah upon us: we were stubborn enemies and He joined our hearts in love, so that by His grace and blessings we have become brothers and sisters.

(attrib. Muslim)

We pray for:
- the victims of war
- peoples made homeless, deprived of citizenship, physically or mentally wounded
- those in mental and emotional conflict
- those who bear burdens for others
- the dispersed. rejected, blamed – by others and themselves

God of nations, whose Kingdom rules over all, have mercy on our broken and divided world. Shed abroad your peace in the hearts of men and women and banish from them the spirit that makes for war. Make the sufferings of our enemies intolerable to us and send us your Spirit for the binding up of each other's wounds. May our pain be joined with theirs, so that together we may be part of the fullness of Christ's own suffering for us.

(Christian)

Let us pray that all living beings realize that they are all brothers and sisters, nourished from the same source of life. Let us pray that we ourselves cease to be the cause of suffering to each other.

(Buddhist)

3. Acting Justly

Maintain the rights of the poor and oppressed

(Psalm 82 v 3)

O people of Justice, let the brightness of the fire of your love fuse and unify the contending peoples and kindreds of the earth.

(Baha'i)

We pray for:
- the victims of harsh and unjust government
- those discriminated against or exploited, socially, politically or legally
- people who are tempted to act selfishly and without regard for the rights of others
- political prisoners throughout the world
- the precious ability to forgive and be forgiven

Did he not find you an orphan and give you shelter?
Did he not find you in error and guide you?
Did he not find you poor and enrich you?
Therefore do not wrong the orphan, nor chide away the beggar

(Muslim, Qu'ran ch. 23)

God of compassion in a world of darkness, remember those who gave light to the persecuted. May thy peace and comfort surround all thy children in this world and in the world to come. Human judgement ends with death, but thou art ever the judge, in time and eternity. Meanwhile let us love peace and pursue it.

(Jewish)

4. Stewarding

He commanded and they were created

(Psalm 148 v 5)

Almighty God, maker of all living things, in whose Fatherly wisdom we trust and depend. Enable us, by the power of your Holy Spirit, to recognise the works of your hand in all things. Grant us, O God, humble and contrite hearts and a clear vision of your purpose for us in our world, that we may become faithful stewards of your wondrous creation.

(Christian)

We pray for:
- those who suffer from the way that the world's resources are distributed
- an end to over-exploitation of natural resources for financial profit
- greater respect shown to the other species who share their world with us
- a more thoughtful and responsible stewardship of time, our own and nature's
- people caught up in natural disasters

May there be peace in the higher regions;

may there be peace in the firmament;

may the waters flow peacefully;

may the herbs and plants grow peacefully;

may all the divine powers bring unto us peace.

The supreme Lord is peace.

May we all be in peace and only peace, peace and only

peace; and may that peace come into each of us.

Peace…Peace…Peace

(Hindu)

Each of the creatures is a sign of God, and it was by the grace of
the Lord and his power that each did step into the world

(Baha'i,Abdu'l-Baha)

5. Honouring

I will deliver him and honour him

(Psalm 91 v 15)

Let the whole universe be blessed, let all beings be engaged in on another's well-being. Let all weaknesses, sickness and faults be diminished and vanish. Let everyone, everywhere, be blissful and at peace.

(Jain)

We pray for:
- an end to social, political and religious exploitation
- a living sense of other people's value, in themselves and not only for our benefit
- a strengthened resolve to choose negotiation rather than force, peace rather than violence, in all our dealings with other people and nations
- respect for ideas and opinions which cut across our own
- the desire to learn and to share; to reach in fellowship across barriers which divide us

Lord of peace, be with those who guide the destinies of the world, so that an end may come to boasting and vainglory and the reign of arrogance dwindle in our time. Give them the courage to speak and the humility to listen...

So may we stand upright, freed from the burden of fear and the weight of suspicion, learning to trust each other.

(Jewish, Lionel Blue)

May we, living rightly, come to know Truth so that, abiding in peace, we may bring peace to all beings; for everything is changing, nothing is our own, and not seeing clearly we perpetuate the disease of the world.

(Buddhist)

6. Working Against War

Seek peace and pursue it

(Psalm 34 v 14)

Peace is to be sought by all. If there is war the religious will seek to establish peace. The Lord has ordained peace, and no-one can engage in war without endangering the stability of the world.

(attrib. Muslim)

We pray for:
- peacemakers everywhere
- the work of advocates and mediators in conflict resolution
- the movement to ban the sale and deployment of weapons
- education for peace throughout the world
- the redeployment of resources, away from war and towards peace

We pray, O God, for wisdom and will, for courage to do and to become, not only to gaze with helpless yearning as though we had no strength - so that our land may be safe, and our lives may be blessed.

(Jewish)

We are going to have to create a new language of prayer, out of something which transcends all our traditions and comes out of the immediacy of love.

(Christian, Thomas Merton)

7. Easing Burdens

I removed the burden from their shoulders

(Psalm 81 v 6)

Teach me, Lord, that life is one in all, so that I may not hurt one of my hands with the other.

(Buddhist)

We pray for:
- peoples and nations encumbered by debt
- places suffering from poverty of medical resources and facilities
- families and communities torn apart by war
- refugees and homeless people
- people injured and disabled by violence

O Lord we pray for those who are denied fundamental human rights, for those who are humiliated and oppressed, especially those who are tortured. Our thoughts rest a few moments with them and we pray that thy love and compassion may sustain them always.

(Christian)

In peace while up and standing
In peace even when seated
This realisation makes me fearless
Our Master, the Lord, is our Protector
He knows all that is in our hearts
I sleep without anxiety and wake up without anxiety.

(Sikh)

8. Nurturing

He makes me lie down in green pastures

(Psalm 23 v 2)

Let none deceive another, nor despise any person whatsoever in any place, in anger or will. Let not one wish any harm to another. Just as a mother would protect her child at the risk of her own life, even so let one cultivate a boundless heart towards all beings.

(Buddhist)

We pray for:
- children made orphans by war
- mothers and small children deprived of food and shelter, or medical care
- separated and disrupted families
- homeless people and refugees
- those without books and libraries, whose schools and universities have been destroyed by war

Almighty God, creator and sustainer of all that is truly good, destroyer of all evil; I bring myself, the family of mankind and this physical world in front of you, and experience your healing power of love. You, the perfect One are spreading rays of harmony, peace and happiness over me and all the world. Your healing vision falls on us all, especially those in authority, inspiring us to seek only peace and unity and an end to all suffering.

(Hindu)

The peace of God, which passes all understanding, keep your hearts and minds in the knowledge and love of God, and of his Son Jesus Christ our Lord.

(Christian)

BAHA'I

Thinking about Peace brings to mind grand thoughts of the need for unity amongst the nations, justice, disarmament and international policy, but for me the journey begins with myself. Our actions are the cornerstone of building peace in the world.

To me it seems obvious that I must recognise all others as equals, be open minded and celebrate the diversity in the world so as to be one of the building blocks upon which the body of Peace can stand.

Being raised as a Bahá'i I have always known that despite what I might see in the world around me, we are destined to live together in peace. In a message addressed to "The Peoples of the World" the Universal House of Justice, the international governing body of the Bahá'i community, wrote that, "The Great Peace towards which people of good will throughout the centuries have inclined their hearts . . . is now at long last within the reach of the nations. For the first time in history it is possible for everyone to view the entire planet, with all its myriad diversified peoples, in one perspective. World peace is not only possible but inevitable."

Armed with this knowledge and certainty, members of the Bahá'i community around the world strive to make this promise a reality. Working at every level and in whatever capacity they can, the task of bringing unity and peace to the world is a central focus of Bahá'i life. Bahá'u'lláh, Prophet founder of the Bahá'i Faith, wrote more than a century ago, "The well-being of mankind, its peace and security, are unattainable unless and until its unity is firmly established."

Creating unity will take time and effort, it requires education, spiritual reflection and a change in the structure of our society. The work of the interfaith movement is a vital tool in this process. It provides a space for people of faith, united in their desire to make a change, to explore the necessity of, and diverse roads to, Peace.

Our interfaith forums allow us to use prayer, dialogue and service to build a lasting peace in the world based on understanding, faith, friendship and unity. If we are all able to play our part in creating unity in our own small worlds, then the foundations of world peace can be built firmly and quickly and as promised by Bahá'u'lláh: "These fruitless strifes, these ruinous wars shall pass away, and the 'Most Great Peace' shall come".

Carmel Momen

Week Two

Victims of Violence
The Divided
The Abandoned
Victims of Injustice
The Despised
The Heavy Laden
The Abused World
The Neglected

1. Victims of Violence

They have pierced my hands and my feet

(Psalm 22 v 16)

Non violence is the highest religion.

(Jain)

We pray for:
- peacemakers everywhere
- the work of advocates and mediators in conflict resolution
- the movement to ban the sale and deployment of weapons
- education for peace throughout the world
- the redeployment of resources, away from war and toward peace

Do not fear, he who fears hates, he who hates kills. Break your sword and throw it away. I have been delivered from desire and fear, so I know the power of God.

(Hindu, Gandhi)

O Lord, remember not only the men and women of good will, but also those of ill will. But do not remember all the suffering they have inflicted on us, remember the fruits we brought thanks to this suffering - our comradeship, our loyalty, our humility, the courage, the generosity, the greatness of heart which has grown out of this; and when they come to judgement, let all the fruits we have borne be their forgiveness.

(Found on a victim at the Ravensbruck concentration camp)

2. The Divided

You have taken my companions and loved ones from me...

(Psalm 88 v 18)

May all beings be happy and at their ease, free from pain, fear, distress or enmity; untroubled, well, unharmed, in peace.

(Buddhist)

We pray for:
- divided communities throughout the world
- groups of people of different racial and religious back grounds living next to one another
- all who seek to heal ancient wounds
- those who still cling to old bitterness
- separated and divided families

May I be able to look upon all beings with the eye of a friend. May we look upon one another with the eye of a friend. By this invocation of peace may peace bring peace!

(Hindu)

All in this world are my friends, I have no enemies; - let the whole universe be blessed; let all beings be engaged in one another's well-being; let all weakness, sickness and faults be diminished and vanish; let everyone, everywhere, be blissful and at peace.

(Jain)

3. The Abandoned

Many are saying of me, 'God will not deliver him'

(Psalm 3 v 2)

A place in God's court can only be attained if we do service to others in the world.

(Sikh)

We pray for:
- The victims of war
- refugees and people made homeless
- those who have been physically or mentally wounded or disabled
- every kind of social outcast
- the despised, rejected, blamed - by others and themselves

May peace triumph over discord, may generosity triumph over niggardliness, may love triumph over contempt, may truth triumph over falsehood.

(Zoroastrian)

Thou art the Bountiful, and All-Loving! So may I be a haven for the distressed, an upholder and defender for the victim of oppression, a home for the stranger, a balm to the sufferer, a tower to the fugitive.

(Baha'i)

4. Victims of Injustice

Redeem me from the oppression of men

(Psalm 119 v 134)

The creation of a powerful and just global civilisation, in which the diverse peoples of the world live in harmony with one another and with the natural world, will require a significant reorientation of individual and collective goals.

(Baha'i, International Community, 2001)

We pray for:
- the victims of harsh and unjust government
- those discriminated against socially, politically or legally
- those who endanger their own liberty by protesting on behalf of the rights of others
- peoples and nations kept in poverty by the greed of the rich
- the grace to forgive old wrongs

Those who are closest to Allah's heart are those who walk gently on the earth, and when the ignorant address them as 'fool', they reply 'peace'.

(attrib. Muslim)

Heavenly Father, may your Holy Spirit lead the rich nations to support the poor, and the strong nations to protect the weak, so that every nation may develop in its own way and work together with other nations in true partnership for the promotion of peace and the good will of all mankind.

(Christian, Melanesian)

5. The Despised

He will respond to the prayer of the destitute

(Psalm 102 v 17)

O mankind, We created You from a single pair of a male and a female and made you into nations and tribes, that ye may know each other, not that ye may despise each other...

(attrib. Muslim)

We pray for:
- A living awareness of people's value
- a strengthened resolve to choose negotiation rather than force in our dealings with nations and individuals
- respect for ideas and opinions which cut across our own
- those who reach out across social, political or religious barriers
- real desire to learn and to share

Blessed are you who are poor for yours is the Kingdom of God.

(Christian, Matthew 5 v 3)

Lord of peace, be with those who guide the destinies of the world so that an end may come to boasting and vainglory and the reign of arrogance dwindle in our time, so that we may stand upright, freed from the burden of fear and the weight of suspicion, learning to trust each other.

(Jewish)

6. The Heavy Laden

Praise the Lord who daily bears our burdens

(Psalm 68 v 19)

Come to me all you who are weary and burdened, and I will give you rest.

(Christian)

We pray for:
- peoples and nations encumbered by debt
- places without medical facilities
- families and communities torn apart by war
- homeless people and refugees everywhere
- people injured, disabled or bereaved by violence

He who gives himself as the nourisher of the poor, gives kingdoms to Mazda, Lord of Light.

(Zoroastrian)

In safety and bliss, may all beings be happy; whatever beings there may be, be they weak or strong excepting none; short, tall or middle-sized, large or small, seen or unseen, dwelling far or near, born or yet to be born. May they all be happy.

(Buddhist)

7. The Abused World

The world is mine, and all that is in it

(Psalm 50 v 12)

They shall neither hurt nor destroy in all my holy mountain; for the earth shall be full of the knowledge of the Lord as the waters cover the sea.

(Jewish, Isaiah 11 v 9)

We pray for:
- people whose way of life has been disrupted by others' greed
- an end to the over-exploitation of natural resources for financial profit
- those who suffer from the way that the world's resources are distributed
- greater respect to be shown to the other species who share this world with us
- a more thoughtful and responsible stewardship of time, our own and nature's

The earth is our Mother; the universe our kin.

(Hindu)

Loving Father, we praise and thank you for making animals as part of your wonderful creation. Help us and all people to be kind to animals. Teach the hearts of all with your love, and increase our respect for all your creation. *(Christian)*

8. The Neglected

He heals the broken hearted and binds up their wounds

(Psalm 147 v 3)

Just as a mother would protect her only child even at the risk of her own life, even so let one cultivate a boundless heart towards all beings.

(Hindu)

We pray for:
- those made to feel 'on the shelf' because of age or disability
- children made orphans by war
- mothers and small children deprived of food and shelter or medical care
- separated and disrupted families
- communities and peoples who have been by-passed in the drive for prosperity

He who has extra food should give it to those who have no food; he who has extra carrying animals should give them to those who have no carrying animal.

(attrib. Muslim)

We ask our Creator's blessing on this home and all who live in it. May its doors be open to those in need and its rooms be filled with kindness. May love dwell within its walls and joy shine from its windows. May His peace protect it and His presence never leave it.

(Jewish)

BRAHMA KUMARIS

P eace is energy, a qualitative energy which emanates constantly from the One imperishable Source. It is a pure
force that penetrates the shell of chaos, and by its very
nature automatically puts things and people into balanced order.
The self is a reservoir of vital resources, one of which is peace.
Through connection with the One eternal and unlimited Source of
peace, our own reservoirs overflow with silent strength. In its
purest form, peace is inner silence filled with the power of truth.

Peace consists of pure thoughts, pure feelings, and pure
wishes. When the energy of thought, word, and action is balanced, stable, and non-violent, the individual is at peace with the
self, in relationships, and with the world. To exercise the power
of peace embraces the fundamental principle of spirituality: look
inward in order to look outward with courage, purpose and meaning. The first step in that process takes careful examination of
one's thoughts, feelings, and motives. By opening the window of
the inner self, individuals are able to clarify and pinpoint attitudes

and behaviour patterns which are destructive, causing chaos and peacelessness.

Peace is the foundation, the major building block upon which a healthy, functional society stands. Peace is the prominent characteristic of what we call "a civilised society", and the character of a society can be seen through the collective consciousness of its members. A civilisation can be heaven or hell depending on the consciousness of its members. Consciousness creates culture – its norms, values, and systems – and consciousness can transform culture.

Ultimately, when all minds are focused and stabilized on the One imperishable Source of peace and synchronised throughout the world, the reverberations of peace emitted from the silence will echo, "World Peace is Declared!"

Extract from "Living Values – A Guidebook" (in Honour of the Fiftieth Anniversary of the United Nations)

Submitted by Sister Regina Baumgart, BK

Week Three

The Vulnerable

Human Arrogance and Pride

What Hatred and Intolerance Do

Anger and Resentment

The Burden of Despair

The Legacy of Deprivation

The Scars of Abuse

The Heritage of Violence

1. The Vulnerable

He is my fortress, I shall never be shaken

(Psalm 62 v 2)

Do they not see the birds above their heads, spreading their wings and closing them? None save the Merciful sustains them. Who is it that will defend you like an entire army, if not the Merciful?

(Muslim, Qu'ran ch. 67)

We pray for:
- all who live in fear of war, or dread acts of terrorism
- those who feel they must prepare for violence, not knowing where it may strike next
- people whose job it is to teach others to fear
- those whose calling is to give encouragement to others
- all working together to bring terror to an end by sowing the new seeds of peace throughout the world

You will not fear the terror of the night, nor the arrow that flies by day.

(Jewish, Psalm 91)

I am able to face all types of challenge when I know how to keep my mind clear and calm. And God is always on hand to help if I am brave enough to set aside my negative feelings and worrying thoughts and let myself be guided by pure love.

(Brahma Kumaris)

2. Human Arrogance and Pride

Haughty eyes and a proud heart I will not endure

(Psalm 101 v 5)

Cleanse ye your eyes so that ye behold no man as different from yourselves.

(Baha'i)

We pray for:
- the willingness to value others and to learn from them
- a real understanding of our own weakness
- victims of entrenched attitudes about superiority: religious, social, racial
- all movements devoted to the effort to help people who feel depersonalised
- those who are despised, rejected, blamed by others and themselves

One who you think should be hit is none else but you
One who you think should be governed is none else but you
One who you think should be tortured is none else but you
One who you think should be enslaved is none else but you
One who you think should be killed is none else but you.

(Jain)

Blessed are the believers who are humble in their prayers.

(Muslim, Qu'ran ch. 23)

3. What Hatred and Intolerance Do

I am poured out like water

(Psalm 22 v 14)

'He abused me, he beat me, he defeated me, he robbed me'. In those who harbour such thoughts hatred will never cease.

(Buddhist, Dhammapada)

We pray for:
- the ability to understand other people's point of view
- the ability to listen and to learn
- those trapped in the compulsion to answer violence with violence
- all movements aimed at bringing together different cultures, life styles, aspirations
- victims of the intolerance that refuses to listen and learn

O mankind! Let your object of life be one and the same, let your hearts be equal (in feeling) and let your minds be united together so that there may be an excellent common status of life for all.

(Hindu)

You shall not hate your brother in your heart.

(Jewish, Leviticus 19)

4. Anger and Resentment

Refrain from anger and turn from wrath

(Psalm 37 v 8)

I could see no sort of anger in God, however long I looked.

(Christian, Julian of Norwich)

We pray for:
- the power to use anger creatively rather than destructively
- all the victims of violence, however justified it may claim to be
- communities and families torn apart by anger, who can see no end to bitterness and resentment
- those whose lives are affected by unacknowledged anger
- understanding of the reasons for anger, our own and other people's

Let all dwellers on earth recognize and know this basic truth; we have not come into this world for the sake of strife and division - God forbid; nor for the sake of hatred and envy, provocation and the shedding of blood - God forbid: rather we have come into the world in order to recognize and know Thee.

(Jewish, Rabbi Nathan of Bratzlau)

He that forgives and seeks reconcilement shall be rewarded by Allah.

(Muslim, Qu'ran ch. 42)

5. The Burden of Despair

My God, my God, why have you forsaken me?

(Psalm 22 v 1)

When I am low in spirits and the sorrows of life bear heavily on me, the invocation of thy name, Ahura Mazda, Lord of Light, cheers me and lightens the load of my sorrows.

(Zoroastrian)

We pray for:
- those who are profoundly discouraged, so that they feel no hope
- people who in any way seek to bring hope to others
- nations and peoples who are politically discounted and economically exploited
- individuals who are considered, or consider themselves, to be beyond forgiveness and acceptance
- organisations dedicated to work for peace amid disillusionment and despair

My God, my Adored One, my King, my Desire! What tongue can voice my thanks to Thee? I was heedless; Thou didst awaken me, I had turned back; Thou didst graciously aid me to turn towards

Thee. I was as one dead; Thou didst quicken me with the water of life. I was withered; Thou didst revive me with the heavenly stream of Thine utterance which hath flowed forth from the Pen of the All-Merciful.

(Baha'i, Baha'u'llah)

Thou settest Earthquake in the South - and Maelstrom in the Sea - Say, Jesus Christ of Nazareth - Hast thou no arm for me?

(Christian, Emily Dickinson)

6. The Legacy of Deprivation

I groan in anguish of heart

(Psalm 38 v 8)

Look where you may
He pervades and prevails
As Love and Affection.

(Sikh, Guru Gobind Singh)

We pray for:
- those bereaved of their loved ones by war or violence
- people who have lost home, work, health and hope
- disabled people, and those who are deprived of medical help available elsewhere
- economies wounded and left derelict by war
- individuals and organisations devoted to relieving distress and deprivation; the redeployment of resources towards peace.

We pray for all mankind. Though divided into nations and races, yet all men are your children, drawing from you their life and being, commanded to obey your laws. Cause hatred and strife to vanish, that abiding peace may fill the earth, and humanity every-where be blessed with the fruits of peace.

(Jewish)

Thy name is healing, O my God, and remembrance of Thee is my remedy.

(Baha'i)

7. The Scars of Abuse

O Lord heal me, for my bones are in agony

(Psalm 6 v 2)

Help me to be good - but help me, my Heavenly Father, to make others good.

Help me to play my part, however humble, in the diffusion of goodness.

(Zoroastrian)

We pray for:
- victims of exploitation, whether intentional or the result of thoughtlessness and ignorance
- those who exploit other people - financially, politically, or through emotional pressure - that they may learn a better way
- organisations whose aim is the welfare of the abused
- those who intend to make money or achieve power oblivious of the needs of others, that they may learn respect for the Creation
- rich nations who live off the labour of poor ones

No one wants to feel pitied by another; it is a demeaning experience. A person with the quality of mercy works on such a subtle level that the support they give never demeans or implies weakness in the other person.

(Bramah Kumaris)

Each of the creatures is a sign of God, and it was by the grace of the Lord and his power that each did step into the world.

(Baha'i, Abdu'l-Baha)

8. The Heritage of Violence

Peace shall be upon Israel

(Psalm 125 v 5)

May all the divine powers bring us into peace.
The Supreme Lord is peace.
May we all be in peace, peace and only peace.
Peace...Peace...Peace.

(Hindu, from the Vedas)

We pray for:
- healing for memories of violence
- the transformation of past sufferings
- the power to understand what we cannot condone
- education for forgiveness throughout the world
- those who believe that loving God justifies murdering other people

Hatred is never conquered by hatred:
hatred can only be conquered by non-hatred.

(Buddhist, Dhammapada)

Father we pray for those places in the world whose history has made them the breeding ground of war. We pray for children who are raised to become another generation of terrorists; for children who are taught the ugly lessons of history in order to keep alive the injustices, indignities and atrocities of the past. We ask that the root causes of terrorism may be healed, so that together we may learn better ways of resolving our conflicts.

(Christian)

BUDDHIST

May Creatures all abound in weal and peace;
may all be blessed with peace always;
all creatures weak or strong,
all creatures great and small;

Creatures unseen or seen,
dwelling afar or near,
born or awaiting birth,
- may all be blessed with peace!

Let none cajole or flout
his fellow anywhere;
let none wish others harm
in dudgeon or in hate.

Just as with her own life
a mother shields from hurt
her own, her only, child -
let all-embracing thoughts
for all that lives be thine,

- An all-embracing love
for all the universe
in all its heights and depths
and breadth, unstinted love,
unmarred by hate within,
not rousing enmity

So, as you stand or walk,
or sit, or lie, reflect
with all your might on this;
- 'tis deemed 'a state divine.'
(the Sutta Nipata)

Submitted by Megumi Hirota

Week Four

Forgiveness and Reconciliation
Love and Acceptance
Understanding and Insight
Empathy and Fellow Feeling
Restoration and Renewal
Thankfulness
Justice
Compassionate Sharing

1. Forgiveness and Reconciliation

Refrain from anger and forsake wrath

(Psalm 37 v 8)

Do not fear
He who fears, hates
He who hates, kills
Break your sword and throw it away.

(Hindu, Gandhi)

We pray for:
- those who have been tragically wounded
- people who are taught bitterness towards others
- nations and individuals with scores to settle
- those who cannot allow themselves to forgive
- those who are unable to let themselves be forgiven

Allah does not change a peoples' lot
unless they change what is in their hearts.

(Muslim, Qu'ran ch. 13)

Forgive us our trespasses as we forgive those who trespass against us.

(Christian, Matthew 6 v 12)

2. Love and Acceptance

Those who love me, I will deliver

(Psalm 91 v 14)

All in this world are my friends, I have no enemies - let the whole universe be blessed; let all beings be engaged in one another's well being; let all weakness, sickness and faults be diminished and vanish; let everyone, everywhere be blissful and at peace.

(Jain)

We pray for:

- people who are suffering or have suffered any kind of rejection
- those who have lost their faith in the healing power of love
- people who feel abandoned by their family, homeland or the human race itself
- the stigmatised, and those who suffer because of the rules we make to accept some people while excluding others; victims of prejudice in any form
- divided communities and estranged families

The real truth of all religions is harmony.

(Hindu)

Did he not find you an orphan and give you shelter?
Did he not find you in error and guide you?
Did he not find you poor and enrich you?
Therefore do not wrong the orphan, nor chide away the beggar
But proclaim the goodness of your Lord.

(Muslin, Qu'ran)

3. Understanding and Insight

Give me understanding that I may live

(Psalm 119 v 144)

The essence of religion is the Lord's Name alone
It abides in the minds of the devotees of God
Millions of sins are erased in the company of the Holy
By the grace of the Saint one escapes the Messenger of Death.

(Sikh)

We pray for:
- wisdom regarding the nature of human violence
- an understanding of our own limitations
- discernment to choose the path that leads to peace
- awareness of the violence that can lie hidden in our own
  well-behaved hearts
- a vision of peace to inspire hearts and change minds

Lord, make me an instrument of your peace.
Where there is hatred, give love;
Where there is injury, pardon; where there is doubt, faith;
Where there is despair, hope; where there is darkness, light;
Where there is sadness, joy.
May I seek not so much to be consoled, as to console;

To be understood, as to understand; to be loved, as to love;
It is in pardoning that we are pardoned;
It is in dying that we are born to life eternal
In thy Blessed Son Jesus Christ our Lord.

(Christian, St Francis of Assisi)

Appreciative of the richness that different opinions and perspectives bring to the tapestry of life, a tolerant person is able to remain calm and contented. When true spiritual love reigns tolerance has no limits.

(Brahma Kumaris)

4. Empathy and Fellow Feeling

I looked for pity, but there was none

(Psalm 69 v 20)

May it please you to bless all peoples at all times and in all places
with your gifts of peace.

(Jewish)

We pray for:
- all victims of prejudice and misunderstanding of others'
  motives
- those who suffer because of other people's eagerness to
  condemn
- those wounded by the callousness and insensitivity
  which changes lives
- people whose behaviour or attitudes anger others
- those unknown sufferers for whom no-one prays

That devotee who looks on friend or foe with
equal regard - such a one is dear to Me.

(Hindu, Bhagavad Gita)

In order to live side by side, it is essential for individuals to have the ability to share the suffering and pleasure of others.

(Buddhist, Nikkyo Niwano)

5. Restoration and Renewal

He leads me beside the still waters: he restores my soul

(Psalm 23 vv 2,3)

Thy name is healing, Oh my God, and remembrance of Thee is my remedy.

Nearness to Thee is my hope, and love for Thee is my companion.

Thy mercy to me is my healing and my succour both in this world and the world to come.

Thou, verily, art the All-Bountiful, the All-Knowing, the All-Wise.

(Baha'i)

We pray for:
- those who work to restore what violence has damaged or replace what it has destroyed
- all who seek to relieve distress of body, mind or spirit, whether untrained or technically skilled
- courage and determination to discover new ways of serving God within his creation
- the precious ability to learn from past mistakes
- hope springing in hearts and lives bruised by war

All powerful and ever living God, in the midst of conflict and division, we acknowledge it is You who turns our minds to thoughts of peace. Your spirit changes our hearts; enemies begin to speak to one another, those who were estranged join hands in friendship, and nations seek the way of peace together. This is our hope and prayer.

(Christian)

We are entering an unparalleled era in history. Never before has there been a global dialogue about the legitimacy or illegitimacy of war, and whether or not we have searched for all possible peaceful solutions. The World Peace Flame helps us to recall that peace is always possible when we make the effort to stand firmly, creatively and with respect for all.

(The World Peace Flame)

6. Thankfulness

Enter his gates with thanksgiving, and his courts with praise

(Psalm 100 v 4)

Before you have finished breakfast
you will have depended on half the world.

(Christian, Martin Luther King)

We pray for:
- individuals and groups of people dedicated to caring for the natural world
- those who take for granted things on which they depend for their own well-being, and ourselves when we do this
- those involved in teaching others to give thanks
- people whose present pain or past suffering makes thankfulness difficult
- all who give heartfelt thanks to God for his loving care

As a flame blown out by the wind
Goes to rest and cannot be defined
So the enlightened man freed from selfishness
Goes to rest and cannot be defined

(Buddhist, Sutta-Nipala)

He did not take my deeds into account, such is His forgiving nature.

He gave me His hand. and saved me, and made me His own, for-ever and ever.

I enjoy His love.

(Sikh)

7. Justice

Give Justice to the weak and the orphan

(Psalm 82 v 3)

I should dispel the misery of others
Because it is suffering just like my own
And I should benefit others
Because they are living things, just like myself.

(Buddhist)

We pray for:
- those who strive for social justice throughout the world
- people bearing the scars of injustice suffered in the past
- victims of inequitable economic systems and
  exploitative trade agreements
- those who risk their own lives by attempting to mediate
  in other people's quarrels
- those who use unjust means in the struggle for justice

It is not enough to pray for peace. We have to work for it - to denounce injustice, not only when it is committed against us, but also when it is committed against others; to defend human rights, not only our own but also theirs; to insist that peace requires sacrifice.

(Jewish, Rabbi John Rayner)

Who could be better of speech than he who calls others unto God and does what is just and right.

(Muslim, Qu'ran ch. 41)

8. Compassionate Sharing

You O Lord are a God merciful and gracious
(Psalm 86 v 15)

Have contentment in your mind
and compassion towards all beings.
(Sikh, Adi Granth)

We pray for:
- those involved in caring for people who suffer
- those who share a loving respect for all living creatures
- all who neglect their own interests out of compassion for others
- individuals and groups dedicated to caring for people in need
- those who need our love

I tell you the truth, whatever you did for one of the
least of these brothers of mine, you did for me.
(Christian, Matthew 25:40)

Let the lovers of God be kindly fathers to the children of the
human race and compassionate brothers to the youth, and self-
denying offspring to those bent in years.
(Baha'i, Abdul-Baha)

CHRISTIAN

Whether it is Christians and peace or Christians and anything else, perhaps it needs to be said at the outset, by way of reminder, that one of the fairly few occasions when we talk about any faith or its adherents as being of one stamp – be it Christian, Islam, or Hindu – is when we speak of that religion or its adherents in relation to another or others. Any one of the major traditions has within it many strands, so although as a priest of the Church of England I hope I speak reasonably representatively from out of one of the recognisable stables within Christianity – I am all too conscious of varying degrees of emphasis and understanding across the Christian family across the ages.

Christians come at the notion of peace (and in my view indeed ought so to do) with hope and joy mixed with penitence and sorrow – and more of that later.

The Christian understanding of peace – like much else in Christianity – emerges from our roots in Judaism. The concept of shalom in the Hebrew Bible is of a peace of which God is the origin and author. It is a multilayered concept, pointing in the direction of prosperity, being cared for, well-being, health, together with good relations between people – whether families or nations.

With that background and context in mind, we Christians

then look to our Jewish forbear and founder, Jesus Christ, through whom we seek peace first with God; then and as a consequence, within ourselves, and then, as a further consequence, in our relating to others.

My own personal definition of Christianity is eight words long: 'The self-giving love of God in Christ'. That constitutes a dynamism which, in drawing us back into the life and purposes of God, at one and the same time sends us out 'in the power of the Spirit' to live and work towards the coming of the Kingdom of God – a reign of justice and peace for all.

It is for that reason Christians come at the notion of peace with hope and joy. But we also come in penitence and sorrow, recognising that in the frailty of the human condition we continue to have conflict and war, within ourselves and among people. Strategies are needed to cope with this reality; strategies that are as ethically and morally consistent as we can make them, with the ideal of which we presently fall short.

At the heart of Christ's way to peace – whether within ourselves or among people – is a self-giving and self-sacrificing love that lives towards peace, whatever the cost, whatever the time frame, whatever the prospects.

Within that inspiring interfaith initiative 'Week of Prayer for World Peace' we Christians endeavour to follow in Our Lord's footsteps, journeying alongside others of differing traditions, differing starting points and emphases and understandings, but together and as one, in the shared pursuit of that peace of which the world stands in such great need.

Fergus Capie

Week Five

Homecomings

Belonging

Making Peace

Working and Living Together

Peace as a Gift

Peace and Justice

Reconciliation and Befriending

Peace in Creation

1. Homecomings

I sing for Joy in the shadow of your protecting wings

(Psalm 63 v 7)

Even if I have gone astray I am thy child, O God:
thou art my father and mother.

(Sikh)

We pray for:
- homeless people throughout the world
- exiles and asylum-seekers
- people whose spiritual journey leads them far from
  home
- wanderers who cannot find rest
- those who have shown us kindness and made us
  welcome

So may we be like those making the world refresh towards
perfection:
May Ahura Mazda, Lord of Light, help us and guide our efforts
through Truth; for a thinking man is where Wisdom is at home.

(Zoroastrian, Yasna 30.9)

This son of mine was dead and is alive again; he was lost and is found.

(Christian, Luke 15 v 24)

2. Belonging

You alone O Lord make me dwell in safety

(Psalm 4 v 8)

Blessed art Thou, O Lord our God, King of the Universe, who hast created joy and gladness, bridegroom and bride, mirth and exultation, pleasure and delight, love, brotherhood, peace and fellowship. Thou Lord art with me, and I will not fear.

(Jewish)

We pray for:
- those who feel themselves to be outsiders, excluded from belonging
- those who treat others as outsiders and refuse to accept them into fellowship
- those who are socially disadvantaged
- people who feel themselves to be inferior and undeserving because of who they are and what they have done
- people who consider themselves to be members of an élite set above and apart from their fellow women and men

I pray that those who hurt me will find kindness in their hearts. I pray for their happiness. I pray that whatever happens my heart will always be full of tenderness and consideration for others. We have all we need so that we do not need anything else.

(Buddhist)

O God, make me live lowly and die lowly and rise from the dead among the lowly.

(attrib. Muslim)

3. Making Peace

Righteousness and peace kiss one another

(Psalm 85 v 10)

I gave amity to all and enmity to none. Know that violence is the real cause of all miseries in the world: violence is the knot of bondage. Do not injure any living being.

(Jain)

We pray for:
- the resolve to avoid war at all costs
- people who excuse war by claiming it as a pre-requisite for peace
- those swept up in violence against their will
- all whose efforts to make peace expose them to attacks from both sides
- all who work for peace and reconciliation

The first lesson on the path to becoming a peacemaker is to stop being at war with myself. When I have learned to be gentle with myself, I can be the same with others.

(Brahma Kumaris)

Continually remind us Lord that it is not peace lovers who are blessed but peacemakers. Use us to combat evil wherever we find it; but give us strength to use life giving, not life destroying, tactics.

(Christian, D Ben Rees)

4. Working and Living Together

Unless the Lord builds the house, its builders labour in vain

(Psalm 127 v 1)

O mankind, we have created you all out of a male and a female and have made you into nations and tribes, so that you might come to know one another.

(Muslim, Qu'ran ch.19)

We pray for:
- a genuine commitment to one another's welfare
- lonely and isolated people wherever they may be
- people turned in upon themselves by cruelty or neglect
- victims of violence or persecution
- those who support regimes of racial or religious oppression

The time is right for us to harness the forces of human unity. In the process, I believe leaders of this course of action will discover a source of unlimited personal power.

(Mansukh Patel, Co-founder of the World Peace Flame Project)

Let us pray that all living beings realise that they are all brothers and sisters, all nourished from the same source of life. Let us pray that we ourselves cease to be the cause of suffering to each other. Let us pray for the establishment of peace in our hearts and on earth.

(Buddhist, Thich Nhat Hahn)

5. Peace as a Gift

The Lord blesses his people with peace

(Psalm 29 v 11)

Suffering and sorrow do not touch those who have the Support of
the Name of the Lord. Grasping him by the arm, the Guru lifts
them up and out, and carries them across to the other side.

(Sikh)

We pray for:
- all in pain or distress
- those who are anxious about people they love
- people whose thoughts are centred upon themselves
- those who feel defeated by problems which seem
  insoluble
- the weary and discouraged

One of the best ways to remain light, even in the midst of chaos
and heaviness, is to keep a conversation going with God.

(Brahma Kumaris)

O Supreme Spirit! Lead us from untruth to truth; from darkness to
light; from death to immortal bliss.

(Hindu)

6. Peace and Justice

Righteousness and justice are the foundation of your throne

(Psalm 89 v 14)

Whatever you wish that men should do to you, do so to them, for this is the Law and the Prophets.

(Christian, Matthew 7 v 12)

We pray for:
- people who have been unjustly treated
- victims of any kind of prejudice
- those whose lives are dominated by the knowledge that they have received unjust treatment
- all who work for social, racial or religious justice throughout the world
- forgiveness for the injustice for which we are responsible

What does the Lord require of you but to do justice and to love kindness, and to walk kindly with your God?

(Hebrew, Micah 6 v 8)

The Bodhisattva ('Buddha-to-be') should adopt the same attitude towards all beings, his mind should be even towards all beings; he should not handle others with an uneven mind.

(Buddhist) Perfection of Wisdom in Eight Thousand Lines, 321-322

7. Reconciliation and Befriending

How good and pleasant it is when brothers live together in unity

(Psalm 133 v 1)

My God, my Adored One, my King, my Desire! I was heedless, Thou didst awaken me; I had turned back from Thee, Thou didst graciously aid me to turn towards Thee.

(Baha'i, Baha'u'llah)

We pray for:
- people at enmity with one another
- those who are at war with themselves
- all who are constrained by deliberately preserved disputes and differences
- victims of inherited prejudices
- people whom we ourselves criticise, devalue or avoid

The more I develop the habit of only holding onto the goodness in others, the more my own sense of well-being will rise.

(Brahma Kumaris)

He that forgives and seeks reconcilement shall be rewarded by Allah.

(Muslim, Qu'ran ch.42)

8. Peace in Creation

We are the people of his pasture, the flock under his care

(Psalm 95 v 7)

O this beauty of the Universe. How did you, my Lord, come to create it? In what outburst of ecstasy Allowed your Being to be manifested?

(Hindu, Dadui)

We pray for:
- respect for the natural world and delight in its wonder and richness
- agencies and individuals devoted to conserving nature
- a change of heart for those who abuse nature for commercial purposes
- a growing sensitivity to the spiritual resonance of nature
- people whose experience of the natural world has been impoverished

God is in the water, God is in the dry land, God is in the heart. God is in the forest, God is in the mountain, God is in the cave. Thou art in the tree, Thou art in its leaves, Thou art in the earth, Thou art in the firmament.

(Sikh: Govind Singh)

They will neither hurt nor destroy in all my holy mountain.

(Hebrew, Is. 65 v 25)

HINDU

O Lord, The fulfiller of all our desires, you pervade everything animate and inanimate. You are resplendent in this material world which we describe in words. You gather and collate all the resources necessary for our survival. Please grant us material wealth and divine qualities.

O citizens! Live in harmony and concord with each other. Be organised and co-operative. Speak with one voice and make your resolutions with one mind. As our ancient saints and seers, leaders and preceptors, have performed their duties righteously, similarly, may you not falter in executing your duties.

O mankind! Let the object of your thought be the same, the place of your assembly ought to be common, your mind should be of one accord and let your hearts be united together: I (God) initiate you in the common inspired hymn and provide all of you with common objects for accepting and offering.

O mankind, Let your object of life be one and the same, let your hearts be equal (in feeling) and let your minds be united together so that there may be an excellent common status of life for all.

Let there be peace in the heavenly region, peace in the atmosphere; let there be peace on the earth, coolness in the waters; let the medicinal herbs be healing, the plants be peace giving; let there be peace in the celestial objects and perfection in eternal knowledge; let everything in the universe be peaceful, so peace may pervade everywhere. May that peace come to me! Let there be peace, peace and peace everywhere.

Submitted by O P Sharma

Week Six

Feeling Useless
Feeling Isolated
Feeling Guilty
Feeling Frightened
Feeling Unloved
Feeling Weary
Feeling Discouraged
Feeling Hopeless

1. Feeling Useless

Be merciful to me Lord for I am faint

(Psalm 6 v 2)

If you desire to listen to the thunderous voice of the Dharma, exhaust your words, empty your thoughts, for then you may come to recognize this One Essence.

(Buddhist, Zen)

We pray for:
- people who feel that their life is without purpose or direction
- men and women who are reduced and de-skilled by changes within society
- those whose contribution to the way things are done or organised is ignored and undervalued
- people who undervalue themselves
- those without love or respect for the humble or disabled

When the heart is hard and parched up, come upon me with a shower of mercy. When grace is lost from life, come with a burst of song.

(Hindu, Rabindranath Tagore)

Take my life and let it be Consecrated, Lord to Thee.

(Christian, Frances Ridley Havergal)

2. Feeling Isolated

I am always with you

(Psalm 73 v 23)

May the stream of my life flow into the river of righteousness.

(Hindu, Rig-Veda)

We pray for:
- socially isolated people, that they may feel close to others in heart and mind
- those who feel cut off from others by what they themselves have done or said
- people who are estranged from or alienated by those who were once close to them
- outcasts and those considered unsuitable for the society of others
- those who feel isolated because of the loss of people whom they love

Help me Ahura Mazda, Lord of Light, to discern the signs of the Age we live in and be in harmony with it, for the world is surging with new life...

(Zoroastrian)

No man is an island, entire in itself; every man is a piece of the continent, a part of the main.   *(Christian, John Donne)*

3. Feeling Guilty

According to your mercy think on me

(Psalm 25 v 7)

I forgive all beings. Let all living beings forgive me.

(Jain)

We pray for:
- those who are conscious of harm done to others
- people who feel implicated in harm done to them
- nations and peoples unable to forgive
- all whose vocation is to mediate forgiveness and acceptance
- ourselves, when feelings of guilt are turned outwards in harsh judgement towards our fellows

All that we ought to have thought and have not thought;
All that we ought to have said and have not said;
All that we ought to have done and have not done;
All that we ought not to have thought and yet have thought;
All that we ought not to have said and yet have said;
All that we ought not to have done and yet have done;
For thoughts, words and works, pray we, O God, for forgiveness and repent with penance.

(Zoroastrian)

Though a man be soiled with the sins of a lifetime, let him but love me, rightly resolved in utter devotion: I see no sinner. That man is Holy.

(Hindu, The Bhagavad-Gita)

4. Feeling Frightened

He who watches over you will not slumber

(Psalm 121 v 3)

You are my father, you are my mother
You are my relative, you are my brother
You are my saviour everywhere
So why and of whom shall I be afraid?

(Sikh, Adi Granth)

We pray for:
- frightened people, whatever it may be that terrifies them
- those who frighten others, for whatever reason
- all victims of terrorism
- those who face the future with trepidation
- situations in which fear gives rise to violence

God is always at hand to help me if I am brave enough to set aside negative feelings and worrying thoughts and let myself be guided by pure love.

(Brahma Kumaris)

It is I. Don't be afraid.

(Christian, John 6:20)

5. Feeling Unloved

The Lord gathers the exiles of Israel

(Psalm 147 v 2)

O my servants, all of you are hungry except for those I have fed,
so seek good of me and I shall feed you.

(Muslim, the Hadith)

We pray for:
- neglected people, all who feel that they are passed over
  and ignored
- people who feel they have no way of influencing those
  on whom their welfare and livelihood depends
- individuals, groups and agencies who work to help the
  forgotten
- ourselves, when we reject the love offered to us

I will not leave you orphaned; I am coming to you.

(Christian, John 14 v 18)

Associate thou, as much as thou canst, with the relatives and
strangers; display thou loving kindness; show thou forth the
utmost patience and resignation.

(Baha'i, Abdu'l-Bahá)

6. Feeling Weary

I am worn out calling for help

(Psalm 69 v 3)

Jesus said, 'Come to me, all you who are weary and burdened, and I will give you rest'.

(Christian, Matthew 11: 28)

We pray for:
- all who carry a burden they can neither support nor relinquish
- all who labour without feeling they have accomplished anything
- those who can see no end to the work they are called on to do
- discouraged people and those whose life has been shattered or bruised by loss
- those who are expected to do the jobs no-one else is willing to carry out

Cause us Father to lie down in peace, and raise us again to enjoy life.

(Jewish)

Be thou my might, O Lord of light. I grope in the dark; scatter the darkness.

(Zoroastrian)

7. Feeling Discouraged

Take heart and wait for the Lord

(Psalm 27 v 14)

If at any time I begin to lose hope in myself, let me simply look inside my heart and see all the good actions I have ever performed from the smallest to the grandest. When I see how much happiness I have given, I easily remember the purpose of my life.

(Brahma Kumaris)

We pray for:
- those who have suffered setbacks which leave them feeling discouraged
- people who have tried hard and feel they have failed
- people whose life has been bruised and battered by oppression
- the disappointed, for whatever reason
- those who believe themselves to have been deceived and led astray

If we sing to God and hear of Him, and let the Love of God sprout within us, all our sorrows shall vanish, and in our minds God will bestow abiding peace.

(Sikh, Adi Granth)

See how the lilies of the field grow. They do not labour or spin. Yet I tell you that not even Solomon in all his splendour was dressed like one of these. If that is how God clothes the grass of the field, which is here today and tomorrow is thrown into the fire, will he not much more clothe you, O you of little faith?

(Christian, Matthew 6 v 28-30)

8. Feeling Hopeless

By the rivers of Babylon we sat down and wept when we remembered Zion

(Psalm 137 v 1)

Save me, O God, for the waters have come up to my neck. I sink in the miry depths, where there is no foothold

Jewish (Psalm 69 vv 1&2)

We pray for:
- all who are in despair
- those experiencing what appears to be final defeat
- those who are mocked by the people persecuting them
- people contemplating, or committing suicide
- those trying to help them

From unreality lead me to reality;
from darkness lead me to light;
from death lead me to immortality.

(Hindu, Upanishads)

Faith is the seed of victory and the foundation of making the impossible possible.

(Brahma Kumaris)

JEWISH

The Hebrew word "Shalom" is used by many Jews but particularly by Israelis meaning either "Hello" or "Goodbye". It is sometimes suggested that Jews do not know if they are coming or going! The Talmud refers to a certain Rabbi Baruqa of Huza who asked the prophet Elijah "Is there anyone among all these people who will have a share in the World to Come?" Elijah answered, "There is none." Later, two men came to the market place, and Elijah said to Rabbi Baruqa "These two will have a share in the world to come". Rabbi Baruqa asked the newcomers, "What is your occupation?" They replied, "We are clowns. When we see someone who is sad we cheer him up. When we see two people quarrelling, we try to make peace between them." One can see that Judaism places a special obligation on Jews to work for peace.

It is not merely a question of loving peace or seeking peace but actively pursuing peace. One of the sages is quoted as follows "Said the Holy one blessed be He: The whole Torah is peace and to whom do I give it? To the nation which loves peace!" Judaism does not suggest peace at any cost, however. The Hebrew Scriptures contain many references to battles and wars but there is the constant yearning for universal peace: "And they shall beat their swords into plowshares, and their spears into pruning hooks; Nation shall not lift up sword against nation, neither shall they learn war anymore. But they shall sit every man under his vine and under his fig tree; and none shall make them afraid; for the mouth of the Lord of hosts has spoken." (Mic. 4 vv 3-4; Isa. 2 v 4). When one discusses peace, obviously one must also discuss war; but it is vitally important to know that Judaism places a very high value on human life: "When one destroys a single individual it is as if that person destroyed the world."

The pursuit of peace therefore is one of the most important Jewish values. There is of course much discussion by the Rabbis of what is a legitimate war or a defensive war but it is quite clear that the Torah underlines a basic rule that prior to any military action against an army, Jews must pursue, ask for and offer peace. Allied to this is the Jewish approach to the ecological needs of the environment even when waging war. There are specific detailed prohibitions against destroying trees which yield fruit and surprisingly there is even a prohibition against building a battering ram using wood from a fruit tree.

Psalm 34 says "Do you want long life and happiness? Strive for peace with all your heart".

Sidney Shipton

Week Seven

Safety
Contentment
Freedom
Peace of Mind
Fruitfulness
Building Up
Rest from Labour
A Thankful Heart

1. Safety

I will lie down and sleep in peace

(Psalm 4 v 8)

And they shall hammer their swords into ploughshares and their spears into pruning hooks. Nation shall not lift up sword against nation. Never again shall they train for war.

(Jewish, Micah 4 v 3)

We pray for:
- all those whom war has abused
- people driven from place to place in search of a safe haven
- those living in imminent danger of any kind
- individuals who are persecuted by their own feelings and thoughts
- nations driven into warfare by fear for their own safety

I vanquished the five foes – lust, anger, greed, attachment, pride – by the power of the Divine Mantra. Saith Nanak,"Thereby my mind was illumined and I attained Nirvana".

(Sikh)

I bind unto myself today
The strong name of the Trinity
By invocation of the same
The Three in One and One in Three.

(Christian, 'St Patrick's Breastplate')

2. Contentment

Blessed are those whose strength is in you

(Psalm 84 v 5)

We praise thee with our thoughts, O God. We praise thee even as the sun praises thee in the morning: may we find joy in being thy servants. *(Hindu, Rig Veda)*

We pray for:
- discontented people, that they may find peace of mind
- those who are weighed down by anxiety
- those whose lives are dominated by responsibilities which weigh them down
- people who work compulsively, so that they find it hard to rest
- ourselves, when we are too busy or preoccupied to enjoy life

Grant that this and every day, we may keep our shock of wonder at each new beauty that comes upon us as we walk down the paths of life: and that we may say in our hearts, when horror and ugliness intervene, Thy Will be done.

(Christian)

I am able to face all types of challenge when I know how to keep my mind clear and calm. *(Brahma Kumaris)*

3. Freedom

I will walk about in freedom

(Psalm 119 v 45)

Let me love Thee so that honour, riches and pleasures of the world may seem unworthy even of hatred – may be not even encumbrances.

(Christian - Coventry Patmore)

We pray for:
- all prisoners and captives
- those who misinterpret the nature of freedom so that their lives grow ever more restricted
- people frightened by others' liberty
- those who suffer from addictions or habits they long to break
- people and nations enslaved by the past

There shall be no compulsion in religion.

(Muslim, Qu'ran ch. 2)

Is not this the kind of fasting I have chosen – to loose the chains of injustice and untie the cords of the yoke, to set the oppressed free and break every yoke?

(Jewish, Isaiah 58 v 6)

4. Peace of Mind

May there be peace within your walls and security within your
citadels

(Psalm 122 v 7)

Give to Nanak, as to the cuckoo the raindrops,
your grace that he may dwell in the Peace of Your Name.

(Sikh, Guru Granth Sahib)

We pray for:
- every anxious person
- those disturbed in their relationships with people they
  love
- people with long standing, unsolved problems
- nations living in fear of one another
- those who have an uneasy conscience

Guard me O Lord, from brooding over sin I have committed: let
not my thoughts sink into the mire of my wrongdoing, but free
them to offer Thee the pearl of good deeds. If I have done much
evil, grant that I may balance it by doing much good.

(Jewish, Hasidic)

Peace I leave with you; my peace I give you. I do not give to you
as the world gives. Do not let your hearts be troubled and do not
be afraid.   *(Christian, John 14 v 27)*

5. Fruitfulness

The earth is satisfied by the fruit of his work

(Psalm 104 v 13)

He laid the earth for His creatures, with all its fruits and blossom-bearing palm, chaff-covered grain and scented herbs. Which of our Lord's blessings would you deny?

(Muslim, Qu'ran ch. 55)

We pray for:
- people who work creatively to deepen and enrich the experience of being human
- those who for any reason feel their lives to be barren and unproductive
- those who have lost their sense of wonder at the experience of being alive
- those who give generously to life, that they may receive generously in exchange
- all dedicated to nurturing new growth of any kind, anywhere

O Lord, let us not live to be useless, for Christ's sake.

(Christian, Charles Wesley)

O worker of the universe! We would pray to thee to let the irresistible current of thy universal energy come like the impetuous south wind of spring, let it come rushing over the vast field of the life of man, let it bring the scent of many flowers, the murmurings of many woodlands, let it make sweet and vocal the lifelessness of our dried up soul life.

(Hindu, Rabindranath Tagore)

6. Building Up

Except the Lord builds the house, its builders labour in vain

(Psalm 127 v 1)

Act in accordance with the counsels of the Lord; rise up in such wise and with such qualities as to endow the body of this world with a living soul and to bring this young child, humanity, to the stage of adulthood.

(Bahá'í, Abdu'l-Bahá)

We pray for:
- those who work together to establish community throughout the world
- the transcending of barriers between races and religions
- those suffering as a result of neglect of any kind: physical, emotional or spiritual
- people who are discouraged or regard themselves as failures
- all involved in schemes of, or movements toward reconstruction

Embellished and immaculate is that place where the Saints gather together. He alone finds shelter who has met the Perfect Guru. Nanak builds his house upon that site where there is no death, no birth, and no old age.

(Sikh)

Let us pray in our hearts for a League of Souls and a United World. Though we may seem divided by race, creed, colour, class and political prejudices, still, as children of the one God we are able in our souls to feel brotherhood and world unity. May we work for the creation of a world in which every nation will be a useful part.

(Hindu, Paramahansa Yogananda)

7. Rest from Labour

Be at rest once more, O my soul

(Psalm 116 v 7)

Pursue not the outer entanglements,
Dwell not in the inner void;
Be serene in the oneness of things.

(Buddhist, So-san)

We pray for:
- all weary people
- those who are overworked and exploited
- people who make themselves work too hard, defeating
  the purpose of their work
- those whose life has become an intolerable burden
  through suffering
- those without freedom to live or die

Leave then thy foolish ranges
For none can thee secure
But one who never changes,
Thy God, thy life, thy cure.

(Christian, Henry Vaughan)

Blessed art thou, O Lord our God, King of the Universe, who makest the bands of sleep to fall upon my eyes, and slumber upon my eyelids. May it be thy will, O Lord my God and God of my fathers, to suffer me to lie down in peace and to let me rise up again in peace.

(Jewish)

8. A Thankful Heart

Give thanks to him and praise his name   *(Psalm 100 v 4)*

As the rose unfolds its petals to the light of the sun, so help me,
Ahura Mazda, Lord of Light, to unfold my heart to thy light.

(Zoroastrian)

We pray for:
- all whose hearts are thankful for God's love and providence
- those who are more aware of what they lack than what is to be enjoyed
- people too busy getting and spending to give thanks for what has been given
- those whose suffering makes thanksgiving difficult or even impossible
- ourselves, for opportunities of service and fulfilment

In the name of Allah, the most merciful, the most kind,
All praise is for Allah, the Lord of the universe, the most
merciful, the most kind.   *(Muslim, Qu'ran ch. 1)*

We bless Thee for our creation, preservation and all the blessings
of this life.

(Christian, Book of Common Prayer)

MUSLIM

True piety is this;
to believe in God, and the Last Day
the angels, the Book, and the Prophets,
to give of one's substance, however cherished,
to kinsmen and orphans,
the needy, the traveller, beggars,
and to ransom the slave,

to perform the prayer, to pay the alms.
And they who fulfil their covenant, and endure with fortitude
misfortune, hardship and peril,
these are they who are true in their faith,
these are the truly godfearing.

(Qu'ran ch. 2)

And who could be better of speech
than he who calls others unto God
and does what is just and right
and says:
Verily I am of those who have surrendered themselves to God.
Good and evil are not equal.

Repair the evil done to you with something that is better
And lo!
The enemy who did evil to you may turn into a close friend.
Yet to achieve this is not given to any but those
who are wont to be patient in adversity.
It is not given to any but those endowed with the greatest
fortune.
If it should happen that a pointing from Satan stirs you to blind
anger, Seek refuge with God.
Behold, He alone is all-hearing, all-knowing.

(Qu'ran ch.41)

Week Eight

The Yearning Dove
Breaking Free
Taking Wing
Soaring
Wings of Power
Going the Distance
On the Edge
The Dove's Return

1. The Yearning Dove

For he satisfies the longing soul

(Psalm 107 v 9)

Come Holy Ghost, our souls inspire
And lighten with celestial fire.

(Christian, Book of Common Prayer)

We pray for:
- all hearts and minds working for God's will to be done
- a sense of belonging within creation
- the healing of wounds which we ourselves carry along with us
- the wounded people whom we don't know or even know about
- the joy of participating in others' visions and of sharing our visions with them

The well-being of mankind, its peace and security,
are unattainable unless and until its unity is firmly
established.

(Bahá'i, The Kiláb-I-Agdas)

Light without equal, so pure;
Thought of you fills our minds,
Love of you fills our hearts;
We desire to be reborn with you.
Desire for you fills our bodies,
Knowledge of you fills our souls;
We desire to be reborn with you.

(Buddhist)

2. Breaking Free

Surely goodness and mercy shall follow me all the days of my life

(Psalm 23 v 6)

Birds at the mercy of the hawk and the nets of the hunter's
hands are parables – these whom the Lord cares for are saved.

(Sikh)

We pray for:
- the release of imprisoned hearts and minds
- those who feel themselves prisoners within
  their own bodies
- prisoners of habit and addiction
- victims of the demands imposed by other people
- victims of demands which they impose upon
  themselves

Hear, O Israel, the Lord our God, the Lord is One.
Blessed be His name, whose glorious kingdom is
For ever and ever.

(Jewish Authorised Daily Prayer Book)

The Lord is all forgiving to those who are penitent.

(Muslim, Qu'ran ch. 8)

3. Taking Wing

By my God I can leap over a wall

(Psalm 18 v 29)

Lord, put courage in my heart, and take away all that
may hinder me serving you . . . let me constantly
remember that my actions are worthless unless they
are guided by your hand.

(Muslim)

We pray for:
- all who are setting out on a difficult stage in their
  journey through life
- those who fear the unknown in any form
- weary people, and those who feel their strength giving
  way
- people who feel trapped in indecision, and do not know
  which way to turn
- The young and inexperienced whether they are
  individuals, communities or nations

When thou commandest me to sing . . . all that is harsh and
dissonant in my life melts into one sweet harmony – and my
adoration spreads wings like a glad bird on its flight across the sea.

(Hindu, Rabindranath Tagore)

By the grace of your name
May humanity find itself lifted higher and higher;
In your dispensation, O Lord,
Let virtue reign in every human heart.

(Sikh, Nanak)

4. Soaring

I will give thanks to the Lord with my whole soul

(Psalm 9 v 1)

Happy are we who, early and late, morning and evening,
Twice every day, declare: 'Hear O Israel, the Lord our
God, the Lord is One. Blessed is His name, whose
glorious kingdom is for ever and ever.

(Jewish, Authorised Daily Prayer Book)

We pray for:
- a wise and thoughtful use of the joy which is in us
- those afflicted with depression
- discouraged people and all who believe themselves to be defeated by life
- those whose confidence leads them to act cruelly towards others
- all who give themselves at the expense of their own health

Lift up your hearts!
We lift them up unto the Lord!

(Christian)

Action rightly renounced brings freedom –
Action rightly performed brings freedom –
Both are better –
Than mere shunning of action.

(Hindu, Bhagavad Gitá)

5. Wings of Power

He came swiftly, on the wings of the wind

(Psalm 18 v 10)

All around are the signs of your infinity: the bursting
life of countless plants. The unending song of innumerable
birds, the tireless movement of animals and insects.
Nowhere can I see a beginning of an end of your creation.

(Hindu, Bhagavad Gitá)

We pray for:
- those who have been subjected to the selfishness or
  self righteousness of other people
- the disempowered and disabled
- people who feel unequal to a task which confronts them
- those who depend only on themselves and either cannot
  or dare not trust others
- those in authority everywhere

The only true conquest is that effected through the Law of Piety,
(Dharma), which avails both for this world and the next.

(Buddhist, Ashoka)

My soul, death becomes a well-wisher when you delight in the Word of the Lord.

The mind is filled with real and beneficial Knowledge when it is imbued with the precious Name of God.

(Sikh, Nanak)

6. Going the Distance

Your dominion endures throughout all generations

(Psalm 145 v 13)

So this ploughing is ploughed
It bears fruit of Immortality
Having ploughed this ploughing
One is freed from all pain.

(Buddhist)

We pray for:
- all who need help in bearing personal burdens of pain
- those struggling for justice within the community
- workers for peace in the world
- weary and discouraged people everywhere
- people who feel undervalued or unappreciated

The Power of God is capable of finding hope
where hope no longer exists, and a way where the
way is impossible.

(Christian, Gregory of Nyssa)

Homage to you, Breath of Life, in the changing seasons, in the hot
dry sunshine and the cold rain. There is comfort and beauty in
every kind of weather.

(Hindu, Atharva Veda)

7. On the Edge

My heart throbs, my strength fails me

(Psalm 38 v 10)

There is another brotherhood, the spiritual, which is higher, Holier and superior to all others, founded upon spiritual suscepti-bilities . . .

(Bahá'i, Abdu'l-Bahá)

We pray for:
- people who feel themselves at or near the end of their endurance
- communities reduced by famine or warfare
- those who are far from home
- people whose pain never really leaves them, or if it does, keeps returning
- those who do not know which way to turn

How should I pray?
Teach the art of prayer to me, so that I may devote myself to you.
Tell me truly; how should I pray?

(Zoroaster)

May the memory of past destruction move us to build for the future,

May the first two atomic bombs be the last also,

May the first world wars be also the last,

O God of peace

O Father of souls

O Builder of the Kingdom of Love.

(Christian, George Appleton)

8. The Dove's Return

How beautiful upon the mountains are the feet of the messenger who announces peace

(Isaiah 52 v 7)

Faith is the seed of victory, and the foundation of making the impossible possible.

(Brahma Kumaris)

We pray for:
- The flowering of the seed of peace in war-like hearts and minds
- refreshment for those who feel dejected in the effort to secure peace
- the renewal of war-torn places and lives savaged by violence
- those who have not yet discovered their own violence
- ourselves, lest we forget to rejoice in God's purposes

Blessed art thou, O Lord, who gavest
light to the whole world in thy glory.

(Jewish, The Hebrew Prayer Book)

Race to forgiveness from your Lord, and a Garden the breadth whereof is as the breadth of heaven and earth.

(Muslim, Qu'ran ch. 57)

SIKH

God has no marks or symbols,
He is of no colour, of no caste,
He is not even of any lineage,
His form, hue, shape and garb
Cannot be described by anyone.
He is immovable, He is self-existent;
He shines out in His own splendour;
There is no one who can measure His might.
He is the King of Kings, the lordly Indra
Of countless Indras, the supreme Sovereign
Of the three worlds of gods, men and demons;
Nay, even the meadows and the woodlands
Cry in praise of Him: 'Infinite, Infinite!'
O Lord. who can tell the count of Thy Names?
According to Thy deeds will I
Endeavour to relate Thy Names –

He is of no nation, and wears no distinguishing garb;
He has no outer likeness; He is free from desire.
To the east or to the west, look where you may,
He pervades and prevails
As Love and Affection . . .

And yet man is of one race in all the world;
God as Creator and God as Good,
God in His Bounty and God in His Mercy,
Is all one God. Even in our errors,
We should not separate God from God!
Worship the One God,
For all men the One Divine Teacher.
All men have the same form,
All men have the same soul.

(Guru Gobind Singh)

THE PEACE FLAME

The World Peace Flame®

The World Peace Flame aims to inspire people everywhere to create their own unique and valuable initiatives for creating a better world and to take a few moments on a regular basis to stop and think about peace. It aims to help everyone recall that peace is always possible when we make the effort to stand firmly, creatively and with respect for all.

In July 1999 for the first time in history, seven flames of peace were flown across the oceans from five continents and united to create a single World Peace Flame in North Wales, UK.

Lit by eminent peacemakers, carried by military air forces and commercial airlines, the seven flames each represented the highest intentions for peace within their continents. The resulting World Peace Flame thus represents the combined aspirations for peace of humanity as a whole.

Since its inception, more than ten million people have taken candles lit from the World Peace Flame into their homes, work places or communities.

Eternally burning World Peace Flames have been installed in the Netherlands, outside the United Nations International Court of Justice in the Hague where a World Peace Pathway was also established on 27 April 2004 with stones given from 197 countries and regions of the world. This included every country in the world (plus some regions) and, for the very first time, the ambassadors from every country endorsed a joint statement for peace. Eternal flames have also been established in Memphis,

Tennessee, US, within the National Civil Rights Museum; in North Wales, in Sydney, Australia and Cadzand and Venlo in the Netherlands.

The World Peace Flame has been taken into war zones, included in peace negotiations and is present as a quiet witness to peace and healing in hospitals, churches, places of worship and civic buildings around the world.

The World Peace Flame works in all aspects of life: working with politicians, faith leaders, educators and individuals. People from all backgrounds have found that the World Peace Flame has helped them overcome the difficulties in their working lives, bereavement and stress.

The words of this prayer express the sentiments of those who work with the World Peace Flame:

"We give thanks for those of every faith tradition, named or unnamed; for the variety and richness of human spirituality; for our common quest for truth and our yearning for love; our longing for peace, and our commitment to justice".

Submitted by Maggi Brizzi

Week of Prayer
For World Peace

"There grows the Flower of Peace,
The Rose that cannot wither."
Henry Vaughan (1621 – 1695)

Some organisations associated with the Week of Prayer for
World Peace

Anglican Pacifist Fellowship

Anglican Society for the Welfare of
Animals

Bharatiya-Vidyan Bhavan

Brahma Kumaris

Buddhist Society

Campaign against the Arms Trade

Centre for the Study of Islam and
Christian Muslim Relations

Christian Aid

Christian CND

Christian Peace Conference UK

Churches' Commission on Inter-Faith
Relations

Conscience – the Peace Tax
Campaign

Fellowship Party

Fellowship of Reconciliation

Gandhi Foundation

Justice and Peace Commission

Muslim Association for Teaching
Equality, Morals, Altruism,
Tolerance

Integration and Community Services

National Council of Hindu
Temples UK

National Spiritual Assembly of the
Baha'is of the UK.

Nipponzan Myohoji

Northern Friends Peace Board

One World Week, PO Box 2555,
Reading RG1 4XW

Oxfam

Pax Christi

Quaker Peace and Social Witness

Quaker Universalist Group

Religions for Peace (UK)

Rissho Kosei-kai

Roman Catholic Committee for
Other Faiths

Schumacher Society

Sikh Divine Fellowship

Toc H

Three Faiths Forum

Unitarian Peace Fellowship

United Nations Association

Women's International League
for Peace Humility and Freedom

World Congress of Faiths

World Disarmament Campaign

World Peace Flame Project

World Peace Prayer Society